Children are a global
do all we can to insure th
book, *A Parent's Guide to*
help us guide our childre
counting on us to have th
reading this book!

—Bishop T. D. Jakes, C.E.O.
TDJ Enterprises, LLP
Senior Pastor, The Potter's House of Dallas, Inc.
New York Times best-selling Author

If you are a parent, your children are online. They are interacting in social channels with their friends, strangers, and even companies in search of information, recommendations, and entertainment. If you are unaware that their search is happening, someone else will be. *In A Parent's Guide to Raising Kids in the World of Technology*, Caleb Kinchlow gives you the principles you need to understand this dynamic new digital world and how to apply those principles in raising your children.

—Gordon Robertson, CEO
The Christian Broadcasting Network

As both an educator and parent, I struggle with the growing use of social media and technology around me. I see how it often impacts family dynamics. Mr. Kinchlow has provided an easy to understand explanation of our digital world. The insightful questions provoke conversation that will put family members on the same side of the digital divide.

—Rebecca Jaramillo
Senior Communications Program Manager
National Institute of Aerospace

All generations going forward will be brought up in a digital world, and Kinchlow's guide is a thoughtful, honest navigation through this ever-evolving landscape. Rooted in research but written for real life, *A Parent's Guide …* offers food for thoughtful discussion between family members, and perhaps an examination of our own tech habits and motivations.

—Janet Sudnik
Communications Specialist
NASA

Caleb Kinchlow provides the discerning parent with invaluable insights into the world of social media and technology...a world most parents don't even realize exists. This book is an invaluable tool for raising healthy children in an ever increasingly chaotic world.

—**Wade B. Mumm**, PhD
Lead Pastor, TV Host and author of
"A Dad's Many Hats"

Technology has embedded itself in our world, our culture, and our homes. Helping our children learn how to recognize the myriad of opportunities and benefits, and at the same time avoid the pitfalls and negative influences, means we HAVE to lead the way. Caleb helps define what our role in that looks like. Whether you are a "techie" or not, this book will help you navigate the challenges of technology for your family.

—**Terry Meeuswen**,
Co-host of The 700 Club, Founder Orphan's Promise

Kinchlow's insights are a masterful work of genius. He has a gift for shining a light on topics that are meaningful and relevant to every generation. *A Parent's Guide...* takes an in-depth look on a topic that has become increasingly more difficult for parents to navigate with their children. Learning to set boundaries in regards to technology and social media can be tricky. Kinchlow's book provides the practical tools and resources parents need in order to gain a clearer understanding of the mediums and to learn to have the right conversations about the ever-changing media at our fingertips.

—**Roxane Griner**
Communication & Production Specialist

Parents can no longer be Luddites while their kids engage daily with the latest technology. The two worlds are intertwined for infinity, either parents can get on board or watch their children and the world move forward without them. *A Parent's Guide to Raising Your Kids in the World of Technology*, by Caleb Kinchlow is the perfect way for hesitant parents to get acclimated to the latest in tech and stay ahead of the game that their kids have already perfected.

—**April Woodard**
Emmy nominated TV Host/Professor of Communication

Parents, Kids & Technology

A Parent's Guide to Raising Your Kids

in the World of Technology

Caleb Kinchlow

Parents, Kids & Technology
A Parent's Guide to Raising Your Kids in the World of Technology

ISBN: 978-0-9794586-7-5

Vincom Publishing Co.

(918) 254-1276
gevinnett@aol.com

Cover Design: Chris Jaen
Cjaengraphics@gmail.com

Text Design: Lisa Simpson
www.SimpsonProductions.net

Editorial Director: Dr. Larry Keefauver
www.doctorlarry.org

GetMyNewBook.com
(918) 361-6654
GVP-4575

Printed in the United States of America

Dedication

My parents, Nigel and Heather Kinchlow, thank you for the years of sacrifice and instilling in me a guiding sense of purpose from childhood to adulthood.

To my wife, Amanda,

You are my constant inspiration and source of encouragement. My forever Valentine, business partner, and teammate who is always pushing me to be better every single day. Marrying you was one of the best decisions of my life. If I had to do it again I would still choose you. I love you to the moon and back, and back again.

Foreword
by John Mason

When I was growing up in the '60s and '70s, there was an issue between parents and kids called the "Generation Gap." That gap today could easily be called the "Technology Gap." That's why I'm thankful for Caleb Kinchlow's timely new book, *Parents, Kids & Technology*. A book that will help you open your arms to change, but not let go of your values.

There are three things we know about the future. First, it won't be like the past. Secondly, it won't be like we think it's going to be. And thirdly, the rate of change will be faster than ever. This is undoubtedly true with technology. As a parent of four children, I have to admit I feel continually lost and left behind when it comes to everything digital. But, even more important right now is, what guiding principles do I need to have between my children and myself regarding social media and technology?

This book answers that critical question. It's full of essential takeaways and principles. Every chapter presents valuable discussion points and questions for us parents to have with our children. If you want the right answers, you need to ask the right questions.

It's easy to find yourself afraid of social media, technology and the seemingly endless bombardment of our children with ideas and actions contrary to what we believe. But every generation has faced these challenges in their own way. That's why the principles shared in this book not only work today but will for the years to come as technology becomes, even more, a part of our daily life. It will be a valuable resource for you.

This is not the time to play it safe. Playing safe is probably the most unsafe thing in the world. You cannot stand still. We must know what to do.

Change is coming at you and me faster than ever. So we should be like babies—they like changes. You can't walk backward into the future. Whether we want the digital revolution or not, every parent needs to know these timeless principles.

Don't allow a "technology gap" to widen between you and the child you love. Technology and thoughtful conversations about the digital world we live in can cause your family to grow stronger and closer to God.

John Mason
Author of *An Enemy Called Average*
and numerous other bestselling books

Table of Contents

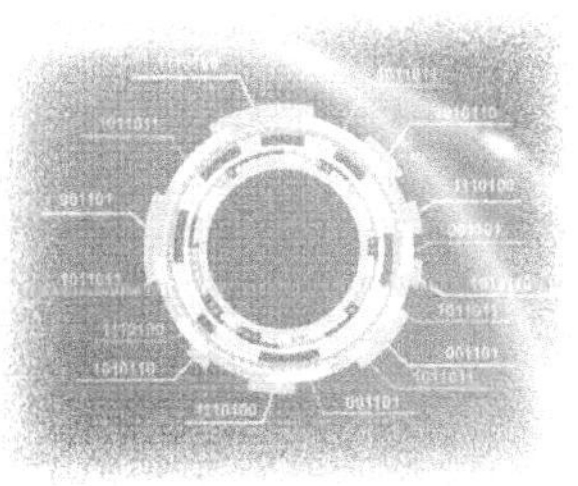

INTRODUCTION

> "PEOPLE CAN'T LIVE WITH CHANGE IF THERE'S NOT A CHANGELESS CORE INSIDE THEM."
>
> — STEPHEN R. COVEY[1]

Social media and technology change at a very rapid pace. So fast in fact, that by the time this book is published, and you have finished reading it, there will already be new apps and gadgets. However, this book is **not** about the latest technology or specific social media strategies. There are plenty of other resources available to stay up to date in that area. This book is about *principles* that will set the stage to help you govern and better understand the mind-set of your teen or tween trying to navigate life while using social media and technology. This entire book is based on a principle I discovered while spending time researching adolescent behavior trends. Through a series of discussions, I was led to this one singular idea that will guide us through our study.

TECHNOLOGY CHANGES,
BUT PRINCIPLES STAY THE SAME.

At the end of each chapter is a discussion section to help you as a parent start the conversation with your teens/tweens regarding "Digital Principles." Make this a family sharing and growing resource.

Let's get started!

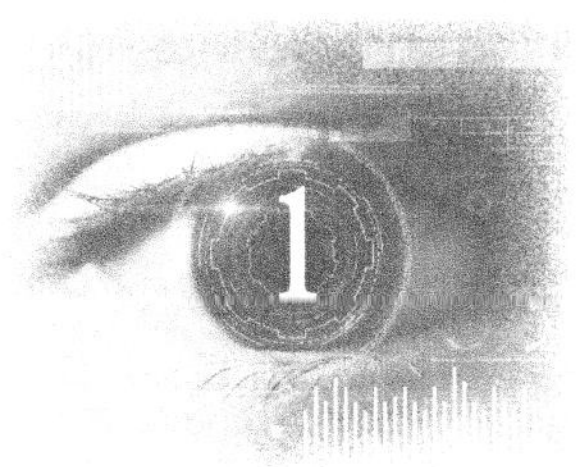

Defining Social Media and Technology

"The PC has improved the world in just about every area you can think of. Amazing developments in communications, collaboration, and efficiencies. New kinds of entertainment and social media. Access to information and the ability to give a voice to people who would never have been heard."

— Bill Gates[2]

Technology is simply a tool used to accomplish a task.

"Social media uses web-based technologies, desktop computers, and mobile technologies (e.g., smartphones and tablet computers) to create highly interactive platforms through which individuals, communities, and organizations can share, co-create, discuss, and modify user-generated content or premade content posted online. They introduce substantial and pervasive changes to communication between businesses, organizations, communities, and individuals. Social media changes the way individuals and large organizations communicate. These changes are the focus of the emerging field of technoself studies."[3] Technoself studies, commonly referred to as TSS, is an emerging, interdisciplinarity domain of scholarly research dealing with all aspects of human identity in a technological society focusing on the changing nature of relationships between the human and technology.[4]

To better understand a concept, it helps to look at "the why" or the root behind it. The interesting thing when it comes to the "why" is we must do a brief study of linguistics. This will show the evolution of a word and the cultural influences providing a holistic perspective as we dive a bit deeper down the rabbit hole.

THIS BOOK IS ABOUT GOVERNING PRINCIPLES, NOT JUST CURRENT TRENDS.

Webster's Dictionary says the word "social" has its original roots in 1857. It acts as a noun and an adjective, relating to or involving activities in which people spend time talking to each other or doing enjoyable things with each other.

The word "media" comes from the Latin plural of mediums, "with roots around 1589, usually meaning an intervening substance through which something is transmitted. Mediums were people who communicated with the dead." It wasn't until 1922 that the term took on our most common definition, primarily used by advertisers: "the system and organizations of communication through which information is spread to a large number of people."[5]

Letters, televisions, and phones were all forms of "social" media to express ideas to one another. As technology evolved especially in the early 2000s, the primary tools and the way we became "social" radically changed. The tools we used and our attention spans became faster, primarily focusing on two-way communication at any given time, anywhere in the world.

Today, these social technologies have taken many different forms including blogs, business networks, enterprise social networks, forums, microblogs, photo sharing, products/services review, social bookmarking, social gaming, social networks, video sharing, and virtual worlds. That was a mouthful, but social media in its simplest form is simply a digital platform that allows individuals to communicate and express themselves to individuals or groups of people around them.

> "ON ONE HAND, SOCIAL MEDIA AND TECHNOLOGY HAVE ALLOWED RELATIONSHIPS TO BE ESTABLISHED AND SUSTAINED FROM A PHYSICAL DISTANCE."
>
> —RACHEL KITSON, PH.D.[6]

THE DIGITAL DISCONNECT

> "A new Pew Research Center survey of U.S. adults finds that the social media landscape in early 2018 is defined by a mix of long-standing trends and newly emerging narratives."[7]

The key word is "digital." This is where one of the biggest disconnects occurs for many parents and educators. The first disconnect is to think of digital in terms of simply a new physical device. However, it's not just the device, it's the world this device creates in a digital space to connect people. The majority of people in the world today use social platforms, but often parents fail to realize how far-reaching this new tool has become. It's ubiquitous and has inundated itself into the very fabric of our modern society.

Take a moment to wrap your head around this Pew Research Center statistic that shows in 2018 there were an estimated 2.34 billion users worldwide on social media with projections until 2020 of continued growth. Facebook alone has over a billion active users by themselves. Ninety percent of eighteen to thirty-year-olds are using social platforms.[8] These numbers will continue to grow. The truth is, we as parents must embrace the change and not try and stop it.

Becoming knowledgeable about these digital spaces is imperative to understanding the emerging social media and technology trends especially among tween, teens, and young adults. That is the goal of this book. Stop at the end of each chapter and review the suggested *Family Discussion Points.*

Key Takeaways and Digital Principles

- **Every family member should know what devices and digital platforms all the other family members are using, along with the boundaries for using them.**
- **Media shapes and influences the mind-sets of kids.**

Family Discussion Points

1. What digital platforms are the members of your family using?
2. How much personal information is being shared, especially by the younger members of your family on social media sites?
3. Why is it important to monitor your family's social media activity?

Notes

A Different World You Didn't Know Existed

"MTV DRAMATICALLY CLOSED THE FEEDBACK LOOP BETWEEN CULTURE AND MARKETING AND MADE IT MUCH HARDER TO TELL ONE FROM THE OTHER, OR WHICH CAME FIRST."

—JOGN SEABROOK, AUTHOR OF
NOBROW: THE CULTURE OF MARKETING,
A WRITER FOR THE NEW YORKER

The number one thing I tell parents when discussing *Digital Principles* is to recognize their kids are growing up in a different world perspective in a completely different world via social media than what they, as parents, experienced in their childhoods. The paradox is simply this; a kid's world runs parallel to the "real world" but more times than not it intertwines for your child.

Permit me to explain. A commuter train runs on two tracks. The train represents life experience as guided by each track which is separate, unique, and providing direction. The train receives support and direction from both tracks. A kid experiences both support and direction from the world track of the current culture and his/her parents' culture/perspective/values/mind-set. Which one a kid draws upon at any given moment depends on a number of factors including their needs, peer influence, adult authority figures, media icons, etc.

Through my time working in television production, I have come to learn a concept that every public relations organization and the networks understand: media shapes consciousness, and consciousness shapes culture.

Media shapes consciousness, and consciousness shapes culture.

By that I mean the way we communicate, the outfit we wear, which smart device we purchase, down to our very ideas of identity are shaped by other people who are often total strangers with a financial and cultural agenda of marketing their values, perspectives, and opinions to us through technology.

The underlying truth beneath the guise of being an individual is that you can never be fully objective and step outside of your culture. The sad thing, it appears most people are completely unaware of how much they are being influenced by the media culture. Space here doesn't permit me to give the perspective of kids on how they use social media like Facebook, Twitter, and Instagram but a great source for understanding this is written by a teen on Wire titled: *A Teenager's View on Social Media.*[9] Here is a sampling of comments:

- *Facebook is often used by us mainly for its group functionality. I know plenty of classmates who only go on Facebook to check the groups they are part of and then quickly log off. In this part, Facebook shines—groups do not have the same complicated algorithms behind them that the Newsfeed does. It is very easy to just see the new information posted on the group without having to sift through tons of posts and advertising you don't really care about.*

- *I'm not terrified whenever I like something on Instagram that it will show up in someone's Newsfeed and they'll either screenshot that I liked it or reference it later. The same goes for commenting.*

- *I am not as pressured to follow someone back on Instagram, meaning my feed is normally comprised of content I actually want to see. That being said, I will come back and scroll through an application that has content I enjoy rather than one where I have to find the occasional diamond in the rough.*

- *Twitter is a place to follow/be followed by a bunch of random strangers, yet still, have your identity be attached to it (this distinction will be important later on). Your tweets are also easily searchable on Twitter which is good but not good if you want to be yourself and not have it follow you around when you're trying to land a job.*

One of the movies my youngest sister and I would watch that is now one of my closet favorites is the 2006 film, *The Devil Wears Prada*, starring actors Meryl Streep and Anne Hathaway. The film centers around a young journalist Andy Sachs (Hathaway) who gets hired as an assistant to the cold-hearted

Miranda Priestly (Streep), the editor and chief of a successful fashion magazine, loosely based off the real *Vogue* editor, Anna Wintour.

In one of the scenes, Andy chuckles at the idea of Miranda along with her magazine design team trying to figure out the miniscule differences in a seemingly ordinary "blue" belt for a model to wear. Obviously offended by the young journalist's ignorance, Miranda explains to her the process of how Andy's "Lumpy blue sweater" she picked out of a bin in some "casual corner store" to show the world, "I don't take myself too seriously," was in fact selected for her to wear months in advance without her knowledge of it by the gatekeepers standing in front of her.

And…that seemingly ordinary blue belt was cerulean not simply "blue." What is truly astonishing, this idea is not just in the fashion industry, it's happening in every area media is involved. The small difference is the gatekeepers now have direct influence to the masses, whether you are a fan of the product or not.

MEDIA CONTRIBUTES SIGNIFICANTLY TO SHAPING A KID'S PERSPECTIVE ON ALL OF LIFE. FOR MANY TWEENS AND TEENS, MEDIA IS THE PRIMARY POTTER SHAPING THE VESSEL'S (KID'S) VALUES, HOPES, DREAMS, DESIRES, PASSIONS, AND EVEN SPIRITUAL UNDERSTANDINGS.

Media Sells STUFF to Kids!

In 1982, Steven Spielberg and his company *Amblin* directed/produced the groundbreaking film that your children have most likely never heard of, called *E.T. The Extra-Terrestrial.* The Film follows the story of Elliott, a lonely boy who befriends an extra-terrestrial (E.T.)who is stranded on Earth. He and his siblings decided to help their new friend return home while attempting to keep him hidden from their mother and the government, who naturally wants to experiment on him. The film became an instant blockbuster surpassing, *Star Wars* as the highest grossing film of all time for eleven years until *Jurassic Park* was released.

However, many people forget the backstory on how this cinema concept catapulted another organization. In arguably one of the most famous scenes in movie history, the script called for a scene where a little boy uses candy to lure the alien. *Amblin Productions* saw an opportunity and approached Mars Inc. about a possible tie-in between M&Ms and the film. For whatever reason, Mars declined the proposition. Maybe they didn't like aliens, maybe this concept was too new, who knows? But what we do know, Hershey's recognized the long-term potential of the opportunity and agreed to the deal.

Instead of going the traditional route of advertising, Hershey did not pay to have Reese's Pieces used in *E.T.* but instead agreed to a tie-in between the movie and the candy after the film was released. A deal was inked wherein Hershey Foods agreed to promote *E.T.* with one million dollars of advertising; in return, Hershey could use *E.T.* in its own ads. No one could have predicted within two weeks of the movie's premiere; Reese's Pieces sales went through the roof.

After candy sales experienced around an 85 percent jump, marketers realized how much people could be influenced by connecting a brand with a story. And with that, quality product placement was born! It didn't stop there; a few other notable companies did similar tactics. For example,[10]

> *Exxon paid $300,000 for its name to appear in Days of Thunder, Pampers paid $50,000 to be featured in Three Men and a Baby, according to Danny Thompson, president of Creative Entertainment Services, in a 1993 New York magazine interview. The same article quotes Joel Henrie, a partner at Motion Picture Placement, as saying: "Look what happened to Hermes scarves after Basic Instinct, Ray-Ban sunglasses after Risky Business."*

Why else do you think advertising for the first Super Bowl in 1967 cost only $42,000, but in 2018 $5,000,000? Again, for 30 seconds...30 seconds! By the way, in case you're wondering that breaks down to $166,666 per second. The point is…

WHATEVER IS BEFORE YOUR EYES BECOMES YOUR REALITY AND PERCEPTION.

Now with all of that in mind, understand that YouTube, the video sharing platform owned by the media giant *Google*, has over **300 hours of user-generated video uploaded every minute and climbing** (2019), and *Facebook* reaches in the billions...yes, billions. That is a lot to take in but let's take it further. Without you doing anything but scrolling on your mobile device, all of this content is targeted specifically to your interest, race, nationality, location, sexuality, and even your previous searches, whoa...that's scary, talk about a real-life Big Brother (George Orwell's *1984*).

When a teen stumbles upon something interesting via online targeting, in less than ten seconds that teen feels compelled to interact or share it with the world. It's not a complicated notion especially when you think outside of social media. If we have a great meal, read a good book, or meet an interesting person, we talk to other people about it and share those experiences. Now, the only difference is the ability to share can be instantaneous with a community of like-minded individuals literally across the world.

Let's break this down to a basic psychological principle. This applies to everyone using social media, but for our purposes let's just talk about your kids. Teens today (born during or after the 2000's) are digital natives, meaning they have grown up with this new form of technology as part of their lives. According to research, on average teens spend upwards toward 7 1/2 hours a day consuming media, and text an average of sixty times a day. As our technology becomes smaller, more affordable, and integrated with our bodies these numbers will continue to increase.[11]

Why Do We Spend So Much Time Online?

Let's look at the reason behind what I call, "perpetual self-reassurance." If we're spending time doing something, to our own minds there must be some sort of value to it. Why? Because we spent time on it. The conclusion is, we wouldn't waste our own time; therefore, if I'm spending time on something it's valuable. We basically weigh or create the value based upon the measuring stick of ourselves, and if something is worth "value" it must be worth sharing it with other people.

The problem is that teens are "always" plugged in spending time online, which means there are a lot of things that pique their interest and need to be shared. People like free stuff. It's just a fact of life and app developers know how to use that to their advantage. Video Game Developers make a free game that is interesting and fun to play. Users begin to play it for hours and develop communities around the gameplay. Although the game is free, to be the best player and unlock more features, you must spend real credit/debit card money to access the premium content.

Naturally, if a person has spent hours upon hours playing, there must be some sort of value attached to it. This isn't just a made-up scenario. The game *Fortnite* has 45 million active users, but made $300 billion from small, in-game $10 to $20 purchases made by users (2018).

Teens have money to spend, here is just one stat that may interest you. "Research compiled from MarketingVOX and the Rand Youth Poll estimates that the total amount of **income paid to teens annually tops out at just over $91 billion**." That does not include money that parents give them.[12]

Key Takeaways and Digital Principles

- **Media contributes significantly to shaping a kid's perspective on all of life. For many tweens and teens, media is the primary potter shaping the vessel's (kid's) values, hopes, dreams, desires, passions, and even spiritual understandings.**

- **Kids are motivated by media to buy stuff. What your kids spend money on indicates not only their needs but also their desires and values.**

Family Discussion Points

1. What is the family budget? What is each family member's personal budget? How are both parents and kids in our family influenced by media to buy stuff?
2. What social media/device is used the most by each person in our family, and how much time a day are they using it?
3. How much time do parents spend with one another without any devices being turned on? Do we need to spend more time together? Why or why not?
4. Examine the areas you have assigned personal value (perpetual self-reassurance) and why.

Notes

What Your Teens Are Looking for Online

"Now the young tend to be presented always and everywhere with what is in a way the most seductive thing there is and that's a mirror. There's a mirror held up to them all the time. It's the mirror as constructed by advertising and TV, but it's the mirror that tells you that you are all there is to be, or you could be, if you bought what we have to sell."

— Mark Crispin Miller
Media Critic and Author of
Boxed In: The Culture of TV

Now that you understand why social media holds such great influence on society, we must state another digital truth. It's impossible to step outside of our own culture that is portrayed to us through the realms of media. In essence, media explores and exposes the zeitgeist (the spirit of the generation). Even those people living off the grid, "unplugged" and detached from the smartphone, are still affected because they live in a society that is shaped by it.

People often ask, "Does media shape culture or does culture shape media?"

The truth is, it's cyclical. There are waves. Remember the principle that whatever is before your eyes shapes your perspective? We can become slaves to the wind of the supposed public opinion even outside of the digital world. The squeaky wheel gets the grease.

When it comes to media, there are two kinds of people: the producers and the consumers. Your child is a consumer. At the current age of your child, they probably don't watch *MTV*, but this *Viacom* company is an example of how their world is being shaped. In the frontline documentary, *The Merchants of Cool*, through interviews with thought leaders, advertising executives, and educators, some of the psychology behind controlling your child is revealed. Permit me to summarize some of what they are saying.

Malcolm Gladwell, Writer, *The New Yorker* Magazine: "Cool hunting" is structured around, really, a search for a certain kind of personality and a certain kind of player in a given social network. For years and years on Madison Avenue, if you knew where the money was and where the power was and where the big houses were, then you knew what was going to happen next. Cool hunting was all about a kind of revolution that sets that earlier paradigm aside and says, in fact, it has to do with the influence held by those who have the respect and admiration and trust of their friends.

Dee Dee Gordon, Teen Market Researcher: We look for kids who are ahead of the pack because they're going to influence what all the other kids do. We look for the 20 percent, the trendsetters, that are going to influence the other 80 percent. A correspondent is a person who's been trained by us to be able to find a certain kind of kid, a kid that we call a trendsetter or an early adopter. This is a kid who's very forward in their thinking, who looks outside their own backyard for inspiration, and who is a leader within their own group.

These kids are difficult to find. So, what this correspondent does is they go out and they find and identify these trend-setting kids. They interview them. They get them interested in what we do. They send all that stuff in. We look at it. We compile it. We look for trends or themes that are happening through all the information, and that's the stuff that we put on our web site.[13]

IN SHORT, EXECUTIVES DON'T KNOW WHAT COOL IS, BUT THEY HIRE "COOL" TO SHAPE YOUR KIDS.

As parents, you can't really blame an advertiser for doing their job, but the problem is the culture says we always need to be connected to the digital world. That's why people can't even use the restroom without taking their smartphone. Their entire lives become a walking billboard for a company that is telling them what to think, how to act, and what is and isn't acceptable. The message here is they must be part of this world. They must follow the rules with blind allegiance that the gatekeepers set for their life.

I remember having a conversation with an employment recruiter at *Facebook* headquarters in Silicon Valley about this very issue. He said that social media (*Facebook*) has changed. It's not just a way to keep in contact with friends; it has become a global marketing tool. To me, this makes perfect sense in terms of advertising and spreading a particular message.

Think about it this way. We freely give away personal information for a service that is, in turn, going to inundate us with ideas to shape our lives, particularly around their product. Teens are exposed to so much information it begins shaping their perspective into what they understand to be acceptable. Similar to a rocks shape being alerted by the constant flow of the current.

Then at some point, those ideas spill out in their text conversation, pictures, videos, and other forms of social media interaction and even their very belief systems of who they are. Even down to the ability to tag a brand in a post, which provides a form of community in something as small as a couple of people who all enjoy eating *Oreos* or any other random act. What a crazy cycle!

Child Psychologist Allen D. Kanner observes, "The whole enterprise of advertising is about creating insecure people who believe they need to buy things to be happy."

The Viacom MTV machine (which really can be subsisted to all forms of media) doesn't listen to the young so that it can make the young happier. It doesn't listen to the young so it can come up with startling new kinds of music. Its entire objective is to listen to young people and sell their own identity back to them.

THE MTV MACHINE TUNES IN SO IT CAN FIGURE OUT HOW TO PITCH WHAT VIACOM, THE PARENT COMPANY AND ASSOCIATES MUST SELL TO THOSE KIDS.

What is the impact of advertising on teens?[14]

Teen-focused brands use a combination of traditional marketing techniques and new communication methods to influence product preferences says Common Sense Media.[15] Here are three key approaches:

1. **Exploiting insecurities.** Brands appealing to teens take advantage of their particular vulnerabilities: the desire to fit in, to be perceived as attractive, and to not be a huge dork. Teens are extremely attuned to their place in the peer hierarchy, and advertising acts as a kind of "super peer" in guiding them toward what's cool and what's acceptable. Both teen boys and girls are highly susceptible to messages around body image, and marketers use this to their advantage.

2. **Tracking data.** Once kids turn thirteen, companies have little restrictions over marketing to them and collecting their data. The information they collect isn't personally identifiable — it's far more valuable. Tracking teens' digital trails helps companies precisely determine their tastes, interests, purchase histories, preferences, and even their locations so they can market products to them or sell that data to other companies. Talk to teens about using privacy settings and

understanding what information they're unwittingly giving to companies.

3. **Using peer influence on social media.** Advertisers actively enlist teen followers on social media to market products, this practice can be seen in any store with an online presence. From high-end to trendy, many brands encourage teens to broadcast their interactions with brands (such as uploading pics of themselves with a particular purse, drink, or outfit). These techniques reinforce the idea that brands "make" the person, and it's essential to help teens realize that their self-worth is not determined by what they own (or don't own).

With the help of well-paid researchers and psychologists, advertisers now have access to in-depth knowledge about children's developmental, emotional, and social needs at different ages. Using research that analyzes children's behavior, fantasy lives, artwork, even their dreams, companies are able to craft sophisticated marketing strategies to reach young people. For example, in the late 1990s, the advertising firm *Saatchi and Saatchi* hired cultural anthropologists to study children engaging with digital technology at home in order to figure out how best to engage them with brands and products.[16]

The issue of using child psychologists to help marketers target kids gained widespread public attention in 1999 when a group of U.S. mental health professionals issued a public letter to the *American Psychological Association* (APA) urging them to declare the practice unethical. Although the APA did not outright ban psychologists from engaging in this practice, as a result, the recommendations of their final report in 2004 included that the APA "undertake efforts to help psychologists weigh the potential ethical challenges involved in professional efforts to more effectively advertise to children, particularly those children who are too young to comprehend the persuasive intent of television commercials."[17]

Key Takeaways and Digital Principles

- **"Cool hunting" was all about a kind of revolution that sets that earlier paradigm aside and says, in fact, it has to do with the influence held by those who have the respect and admiration and trust of their friends.**
- **We look for the 20 percent, the trendsetters, who are going to influence the other 80 percent.**
- **In short, executives don't know what cool is, but they hire "cool" to shape your kids.**
- **The media machine tunes in so it can figure out how to sell to your kids.**

Family Discussion Points

1. Who are the trendsetters among your group of friends?
2. Who has the respect and admiration of most of your friends?
3. What or who is the major influence in your life as far as choices of the things you like and the things you do?

Notes

Death by Social Media: A Real-Life Tragedy

"'After hours of scrolling through Instagram feeds, I just feel worse about myself because I feel left out,' said Caitlin Hearty, a 17-year-old Littleton, Colorado, high school senior who helped organize an offline campaign last month after several local teen suicides."[18]

It's safe to say, one of the roles of a good parent or mentor is protecting and shaping teens and tweens into well rounded human beings, and that includes monitoring what they are exposed to. I don't want to scare you, but the truth is, it's not a matter of if your child is going to be exposed to something inappropriate online via a conversation, picture, or video, but rather when. It's likely your sweet, innocent child playing down the hall in your home has already been exposed.

REMEMBER, UNRESTRICTED MOBILE ACCESS IS LIKE A SEWAGE LINE, WITH ALL KINDS OF CONTENT. A COUPLE OF MISSPELLINGS MIGHT TAKE YOUR CHILD DOWN A PLACE THEY DON'T WANT TO GO.

You might be thinking, not my child, but according to an internet filter company, *Covenant Eyes*, the average age for something like pornographic exposure is eight years old. Ninety percent of boys and 62 percent of girls are exposed before turning eighteen and on social media—evil and dangers abound.

In 2016, *CBN News* reporter Charlene Aaron covered a story about a teenager named Sydney Seller. She was your typical fun-loving young girl who was very close to her parents, particularly her mother, Jennifer. They did just about everything together including shopping, hair, and nails. Sydney was even an altar server at her local Catholic service. Nonetheless, Sydney's social media secrets that she kept from her parents would eventually lead to tragedy.

On December 7, 2014, Sydney's parents found their teenage daughter hanging from a belt in her bedroom.

"It was such a shock that I opened the door and I said, 'Sydney, that is not a funny practical joke,'" Sydney's mom explained. Although, it wasn't a joke or illusion; it was reality.

"I immediately ran into the room," she said. "I didn't have the strength to pick her up; that's when I started screaming for my husband...he picked her up. I cut her down. We laid her down on the ground and he immediately started CPR and I called 9-1-1." But it was too late. Fourteen-year-old Sydney Sellers was dead.

Like most teens, Sydney had been using an anonymous social media app to communicate with an online "friend" on an app called "KIK." The parents were in shock when they discovered the contents of the conversation their fourteen-year-old was having. A conversation initiated by a mysterious person, so explicit that Sydney's parents, married for seventeen years, wouldn't have even had in the privacy of their own bedroom.

The subject was "erotic asphyxiation" or breath control play, which is the intentional restriction of oxygen to the brain for the purposes of sexual arousal.

"I started looking and there was a conversation happening at the moment she died between her and a person who purported himself to be a teenage boy and it was disgusting and he was giving her instructions of things to do."[19]

How to Avoid a Tragedy

These kinds of tragedies beg us to ask, "How could this happen?" Well, that really is a twofold answer. Experts, such as licensed family therapist, Dr. Linda Mintle, put it this way: "They (predators) know which sites kids tend to populate and go to and they pose as someone that a child might easily talk to...Smartphone apps are often the weapons used to target kids."

REMEMBER THAT DIFFERENT WORLD WE TALKED ABOUT PREVIOUSLY? IN THE REAL WORLD, YOUR CHILD MIGHT BE AWARE OF "STRANGER DANGER," BUT ONLINE ANONYMITY PROVIDES A FALSE SENSE OF SECURITY. WHEN THERE IS THE ABILITY TO DELETE OR HIDE A CONVERSATION, THERE COMES A GREAT LIKELIHOOD TO PARTICIPATE IN RISKY BEHAVIOR.

In 2015, a local news station in Grand Rapids was contacted by a convicted former sex offender warning parents about social media messenger apps. The offender showed the reporter within minutes of creating a profile and without contacting anyone, two people—purportedly teenage girls—reached out to chat. One of the teens had a profile name indicating personal struggles.

The sex offender being interviewed said that is exactly what perpetrators look for. "That's when a sexual predator can jump in—like me. I would jump in and say, 'Hey. What's your problem? Let's talk,'" the man said.

"I would be their comfort. I would be their go-to person… The first thing that I thought was, 'Wow! I can be whoever I want to be. I can get anybody I want. I can achieve my sexual glorification through this app,'" he said. "That's when I said, 'You know what, I have to stop this.'"[20]

The stories don't end with those. There are many online experiments of teens/tween inviting other "teens" to secretly meet them, only to find out once arriving to the location they weren't talking to a teen at all. Thankfully those interactions conclude with shocked and tearful parents being in on the experiment. However, imagine how many other young people ended up in much worse scenarios.

For teens, perception is reality in the digital space. It becomes so easy to think people are who they say they are with a profile picture. Teens/tweens have a habit of assuming everyone is just like them. When they are not, they act surprised. Just as kids might think their silly or semi-sexual picture is no big deal or their post is just them having fun with friends, why would they think the person online isn't also doing the same thing? Why would they have a reason to think any different?

Deborah Yurgelun-Todd and colleagues at the McLean Hospital Brain Imaging Center in Boston, Massachusetts, suggest, "While adults can use rational processes when facing emotional decisions, teenagers are simply not yet equipped to think through things in the same way. In other words, their brains, particularly the frontal lobe of their brains, have not been fully developed to adjust and think through some of these life challenges. The frontal lobes of the brain have been implicated in behavioral inhibition, the ability to control emotions and impulses. The frontal lobes are also thought to be the place where decisions about right and wrong, as well as cause-effect relationships, are processed."[21]

What Parents Know That Kids Don't

What can we as a parent share to help our kids understand the similarities in our lives growing up around the same age?

We have covered the scientific portion to answer this question, but to understand the second number in the equation of teens online, let's blow the dust off some memories. Let's talk about emotion.

What are some of the things you remember from your teen to young adult years? Seriously, take a few moments to think back. Think about some of the experiences that impacted you the most. Maybe it was a birthday, a first kiss, the prom. What was it like in school? Who were the cool kids? Maybe you were one of the cool kids.

Now think about how you felt during those moments. You probably shared them with a friend, but you had to call or wait to see them if they weren't close by. What if, through some magic device, you could instantly share your feelings with your friends about literally anything and everything happening within your view, no matter where they were in the country or dare I say the world? That is EXACTLY the kind of world your teen is living in today.

It's intriguing to watch how each generation rebels against the previous generations, whether it is the latest dance craze or music. It feels as if only your peers can understand how you feel. Like no one in all of history ever felt how you feel in this moment right now. Phrases like, "Back when I was your age or back in my day" only fuel the fire that our parents don't understand what it's like to be our age. Although this thought is completely illogical, for a teenager it makes perfect sense, not to mention hindsight is always 20/20.

Oh, the life of a teen enduring those awkward years trying to figure out your hormones, personal style, and social status at the same time. It's the same feeling you might have as a high school senior looking at a freshman, wondering why and if you were ever that awkward. As an adult, maybe it's the same feeling of being one of the senior employees at your job and watching the new young whippersnappers come jogging into the office, starry-eyed and gung ho. This is an observation that continues all the way until you die. These are the lessons that only growing older teaches us.

YOUR FEELINGS ARE NOT THAT DIFFERENT FROM THE PEOPLE WHO CAME BEFORE YOU.

I had the pleasure to be raised during what some would call the "digital revolution," the transition time of rapid growth of technology in the 2000s. The beginning of *Facebook, Google,* smartphones, and opportunities via *America Online Instant Messenger* enabled teens to share their personal feeling with an "away message."

Entrepreneur and Businessman, Daymond John once said, "There is nothing new in this world, just new ways of distribution and that's where social media comes in." He's definitely correct.

As I have matured, babysat my nieces, mentored young boys, and spent time raising my own son, I realize the words, "back when I was your age" made perfect sense. These wise sages, known as adults, were trying to help me understand basic teenage experiences don't change. The only difference is the ability to share publicly.

Parents, when approaching your children, do not approach from a place of condemnation. *Technology changes but principles do not.* Share some of your stories, successes, failures and things you wish you could have done differently.

By doing this, it allows your teen to understand that you weren't always superhero mommy or daddy. For teens, parents tend to be the most stable example if there is some sort of relationship there.

It's not until they reach adulthood, presumably college, that they begin to understand some of the complications adult life has to offer. Let them know you struggled to fit in (or maybe still do) when you were growing up. Share how adults either in your job or through the internet are doing some of the same things and experiencing similar consequences.

THE KEY PRINCIPLE HERE IS COMMUNICATION AND SELF-DISCLOSURE WITH YOUR CHILD.

You are putting yourself in a position as a resource because you have been where they are. From a scientific standpoint, this is a key time period in the development of the frontal lobe. In fact, it will continue throughout adolescence and well into the early twenties. This is great news because as parents you have the ability to help shape that development as they are sharing on the digital stage for all their friends to see.

Shakespeare famously wrote, "All the world's a stage, and all the men and women merely players (actors)." *The Bard* never did express who the audience was, but that statement accurately reflects today's reality. Social media for teens has literally made them all players (actors) standing on a digital stage, performing for each other without a script, and hoping someone will give them applause.

Parents, I encourage you to be both the audience clapping the loudest in the theater, and also the director giving cues of encouragement to these awkward artists in their big performance called life. It's during this time where your teen needs wise understanding, guidance, and encouragement that will shape their future.[22]

Social media and the technology that goes with it are commonplace. Why? As we discussed in earlier chapters, the "why" we provide the technology matters and only you as a parent can answer that by pausing and taking a look at yourself. Maybe because everyone has a smart device and you don't want your kids to be made fun of, or maybe just like when your kids ask you for a new toy, you get it for them just because it's cool and the "in thing to do." Smart devices can certainly be entertaining, but I assure you these are not toys.

A smart device is an electronic gadget that can connect, share, and interact with its user and other smart devices via short-range Bluetooth connection or the internet. The most common form is a smart cellphone. Chances are you have a smart device and so do your kids, but giving your child unrestricted access to the world via a smart device is the equivalent of taking a sewage line and connecting it to them.

Is it really that serious, Caleb? Absolutely! We are talking about your tween/teen, who does not have a license, isn't able to get into a rated R movie, buy alcohol, is extremely curious, hormonal, and probably doesn't have a real job outside of taking out the trash and cleaning their room. Now, they have access to the entire world in their pocket. That sounds like a recipe for disaster if unchecked!

I have never been inside an actual sewer, but from what I have read, people have found some really nice things down there, but primarily there is a lot of filth. The challenge with teens, tweens, and young adults is they are lacking the wisdom on how to wade through some of the filth when it's presented or stumbled upon.

Remember the previous section on the frontal lobe? (page 41) Here is something my mother, Dr. Heather Kinchlow, would always tell me: "Wisdom will go to the future and consider the outcome of a situation before doing." You see, wisdom is the sum of knowledge plus understanding. In order to be effective in engaging your teen, you must take the time to not only know what the technology is but also seek to understand the "why" behind it.

At any given point in a twenty-four-hour period, there are people waiting and willing to connect on a smart device. This applies to adults, but particularly to young people going through that awkward stage of life.

For example, you're not feeling secure about who you are, and someone comes along anonymously or publicly and starts giving you attention. What would you do? I know what I would do and have done. You start going in that direction. It's one of the reason people ignore red flags and stay in bad relationships. A person with low self-esteem is looking for anything to give them value. Teens tend to be less secure but even more so now because their value is constantly being assessed on a digital stage. Whether that's from their peers or self-imposed comparison.

KEY TAKEAWAYS AND DIGITAL PRINCIPLES

- **Remember, unrestricted mobile access is like a sewage line, with all kinds of content. A couple of misspellings might take your child down a place they don't want to go.**
- **In the real world, your child might be aware of "stranger danger," but online anonymity provides a false sense of security.**
- **When there is the ability to delete or hide a conversation, there comes a great likelihood to participate in risky behavior.**
- **Your feelings are not that different from the people who came before you.**
- **The key principle here is communication and sharing yourself and some of your past experiences with your child.**

Family Discussion Points

What can parents offer about their lives to show how their life growing up is no different than their kids?

1. What are some of the things you remember from those teens to young adult years? Think about some of the experiences that impacted you the most. Maybe it was a birthday, a first kiss, or the prom. What was it like in school and who were the cool kids? Now, think about how you felt during those moments as you endured those awkward years of trying to figure out your hair, face, and hormones. Share them with your teen/tween.

2. Parents, when approaching your children, approach them with transparency, sharing about your past experiences, listening, and caring. Remember that communication with your child is a dialogue, not a monologue with you doing more listening than talking! Approach them from a place of a person who has lived out those same emotions and experiences in some form. So, share some of your stories, your faults, your successes, and things you wish you could have done differently. Let them know you struggled to fit in (or maybe still do) when you were growing up.

The Rules of the Real World Don't Apply

"Psychological research suggests effective communication can be summed up in the Three C's of communication: Context, Cluster, and Congruence."[23]

Context focuses on and includes the environment the situation takes place in and the relationship of the individuals involved.

Clusters are what we as people use to prevent us from allowing a single gesture or movement to be definitive in determining a person's state of mind or emotion. For example, crossing your arms at your chest can be a sign of being resistant and close-minded. However, if the person's shoulders are raised and their teeth are chattering, they might just be cold.

Congruence asks, "Do the spoken words match the tone and the body language?" For example, after someone falls and they verbally state they are fine, however, their face is grimacing and their voice is shaky, you might want to probe a little deeper.

So, what method of communication allows you to learn more about another person: a post on *Facebook* or a face-to-face conversation? We connect on a deeper, more meaningful level when we converse with others personally, yet studies show an increased dependency on social media. Why? Social media is a convenient way of communicating, but it lessens the quality of the connection. Almost two-thirds of U.S. adults admit they use social media to connect. Its rise to prominence changes our ability to interact with others on a meaningful level. Our social skills are challenged to the point that many now struggle to interact in traditional conversations.

One survey revealed that 74 percent of Millennials prefer conversing digitally rather than in person. While this helps them communicate more efficiently, it diminishes their communication effectiveness. The more people use digital communication, the more interpersonal communication skills decline. Our need for rapid bits of information replaces our ability to clearly express thoughts and ideas when speaking to others.[24]

Social media's effect on our ability to interact and communicate is visible throughout all areas of society, so what does this mean for interpersonal communication? According to Paul Booth, Ph.D., an assistant professor of media and cinema studies in the College of Communication at DePaul University in Chicago, social media certainly affects how we engage with one another across all venues and ages. "There has been a shift in the way we communicate; rather than face-to-face interaction, we're tending to prefer mediated communication," he says. "We'd rather e-mail than meet; we'd rather text than talk on the phone."[25]

PSYCHOLOGISTS SUGGEST OVER 80 PERCENT OF COMMUNICATION IS NONVERBAL.[26]

When communicating through a device, these factors of communication are primarily erased. So, you can imagine through a digital platform primarily composed of text on a screen, how easy it is to separate the emotion.

In my research, 90 percent of young people feel the interactions of social media are "less harsh." This is due to the lack of tangible emotion of standing in front of another person. Visit any message board, social media page, or YouTube video and you won't be hard-pressed to find hateful and sexual comments.

WHEN LOOKING AT A PIXEL ON A SCREEN, THE CHEMICAL EMOTIONS ARE REAL, BUT THE CONSEQUENCES ARE NOT TANGIBLE.

One student said, "We don't have to see the look in their eyes. You don't have to see the look of hurt that comes out of them. You don't have to feel the pain that they're feeling because through a screen, you say it and you can't see anything after that." Many kids believe...

THEREFORE, THE RULES OF THE REAL WORLD DON'T APPLY WHEN VIEWING AND CONNECTING ON A DEVICE INSTEAD OF IN PERSON.

Unless a person is seasoned in writing and taking the time to craft a compelling emotional sentence, which most of us don't (especially teens who can barely communicate in person), displaying emotion or having a meaningful conversation is challenging to have online. Responses online where they respond with like verbiage often backfire. **They don't show you the pain a person might be feeling.** The conversation becomes a series of back and forth sentences or phrases without emotion, oftentimes providing people the freedom of expression without any regard for the consequences.

If a student is caught bullying or harassing a person online, their page may be blocked or temporarily shut down, but that is about it. In the real world, those consequences would be a lot higher. A student might be expelled from school for bullying, end up in a fight, or experience some other form of retaliation.

In the mind of the teen, it doesn't register that anything on a screen can be captured and printed out, bringing life to their online conversation. Those words can be, and in many cases, have been saved by another person for blackmail or to build a case against them. There are dozens of stories involving teens sending "for your eyes only" photos to their boyfriends or girlfriends that have been screenshot or shared. Some of these kids have even had to register as sex offenders at the age of twelve, a "mark" that can follow them for ten years.

Nicholas David Bowman, PhD, an assistant professor of communication studies in the Eberly College of Arts and Sciences at West Virginia University, says actions that trigger a bad online relationship likely are the same ones that trigger a bad relationship in real life—only the modality has changed. "For example, cyberbullying has largely the same antecedents and behavioral, emotional, and effective consequences as does [noncyber] bullying," Bowman says. "Yet the difference is the 'more'—that is, social media allows for more contact, more communication, and in a more public manner."

In a bullying event, often the person being bullied can remove himself or herself from the environment, at least temporarily. For example, a child being bullied at school can escape the playground when he or she goes home each night. "However, cyberbullying is marked by its persistence," Bowman says. "The bullying messages don't stay in a particular space, such as a playground, but can follow the child home. If we consider that bullying's effects on an individual can build over time, then there is a real concern that increasing contact between bullies and their targets in persistent and digital interactions might exacerbate the problem."[27]

Tragedies of students being bullied online and then in "real" life murdering people have begun to show up more and more. One of the reasons suggested by students is people are inherently self-centered. Due to the lack of the influence of the three C's of communication (Context, Cluster, Congruence) and the illusion of anonymity, a user projects their own interpretations of what's being said or the person's intentions. **You can practically trick people into saying and doing things because it's the internet. Because of the perceived distance from consequences and anonymity, many people say and do things they wouldn't express in the real world.**

Communication online is built upon a perceived reaction. Getting a reaction in response to something seen or said, whether positive or negative, is the ultimate goal. Students say they understand the basics of communication. In other words, they know positive words will reinforce a person's feelings, but negative words do the opposite. However, in the digital world actions don't go beyond the screen, which is really odd because when someone says something to them, it will still be internalize. It really is a strange juxtaposition perspective.

I believe the deficit in perceived control isn't intentional, it simply comes as a byproduct of a world that's designed to give them control. For example, depending on when you read this you might remember the invention of *iTunes* and the *iPod*. Motivational Speaker Jonathan Sprinkles suggests, that kids grew up with the ability to listen to the songs "i" want, whenever "i" feel like it, in the order that "i" decided is correct. This kind of customization lead to believing they had more control in every area of communication in their digital space. If they don't look good in a photo, take ten more to find the right angle. If you're not feeling very attractive, put on a camera filter and change your look a little. If you feel like you want to be heard, simply post a thought online and someone will respond. With this in mind, help them be aware of what their communication says about them and what they can actually control. Your teens should be given an opportunity to express how they feel by making them take ownership and responsibility for the privilege of being granted certain social freedoms.

Key Takeaways and Digital Principles

- **Psychological research suggests effective communication can be summed up in "The Three C's" of communication: Context, Cluster, and Congruence.**

- **Psychologists suggest over 80 percent of communication is nonverbal.**[28]
- **However, when communicating through a device, these factors of communication are primarily erased.**
- **When looking at a pixel on a screen, the chemical emotions are real, but the consequences are not always tangible.**
- **The rules of the real world don't apply on your device...Really?**

Family Discussion Points

Here are a few questions to get the conversation started if your child is showing an interest in social media:

1. How would you respond if a stranger tried to contact you through an online site?
2. Why do you want to be on social media?
3. Explain the difference between good images and bad images.
4. Understand the filters and how the devices work (Google, what does "blank" device do).
5. Establish what information is good to share and what isn't. **Keep some stuff private.** Your name, address, phone number, when you are alone, etc, should stay private. Your hobbies, favorite ice cream

flavor, or pet's name all can be fun stuff to share with like-minded folks online.

6. Ask what they posted on social media.
7. Follow them or be friends online, but don't "stalk" their social media in terms of commenting on everything they post.

My Value Is in Social Media

"A survey conducted by the Royal Society for Public Health asked 14 to 24-year-olds in the UK how social media platforms impacted their health and well-being. The survey results found that Snapchat, Facebook, Twitter, and Instagram all led to increased feelings of depression, anxiety, poor body image, and loneliness."

—Rachel Ehmke
"How Using Social Media Affects Teenagers"
Child Mind Institute

As an adult looking back at my life, it was full of influential people. Most notable were my parents, who told me I could do and be anything. Even my name, Caleb,[29] means "one of a different spirit." Their words and influence as a child became a source of encouragement and foundation that made me the man I am today. This was the first understanding of my value.

As children, our initial value is determined by our family tribe. The home establishes the parameters of our personal value system, which leads to how we see ourselves when interacting with the outside world. This is also the place where we learn what is important in life like character, good manners, and fair play.

As we grow a little older, we desire to understand our value within a social class that is developed with peers. What things do you own, who is the fastest, smartest, funniest, the most popular, etc?

As an adult, it doesn't stop. Eventually, it leads to trying to understand our value in a job which is based on a salary, the home we purchased, the kind of vehicle we drive, how attractive our spouse might be, etc.

THE VALUE IN SOCIAL MEDIA REALLY COMES FROM TWO PARTS, PERCEIVED WORTH AND COMMUNICATION.

It's All about the Numbers

The nature of social media centers around computer codes and analytics. In order to have analytics, you need numbers and numbers equal value.

EVERY SOCIAL MEDIA PLATFORM PROVIDES ONE BASIC FUNCTION FOR THE WORLD TO SEE AND THAT'S HOW MANY FOLLOWERS YOU HAVE.

Simply put, we are a society of consumers. We need to have the most money, biggest house, coolest car, newest phone, etc.

Whenever I speak to a young person about their social platforms, the question that always comes up is, "How many followers do you have?" For the average user, social media isn't just a way to communicate; it's simply a popularity contest. The problem, as we will explore in a moment, is that popularity most of the time does not extend beyond the platform. It is further warped because of the sense of "reality" the platform provides. The truth is, social media only shows a snippet of a person's life, even the "star," people are following.

ON SOCIAL MEDIA, EVERYONE IS A PRODUCT, THEY JUST DON'T KNOW IT.

Posting Chemical Romance

Here is the science behind why we need the numbers, followers, and the likes. Simon Sinek, in a talk entitled "Why Leaders Eat Last," explains it with two chemicals, Dopamine and Serotonin. Dopamine is essentially the feel-good chemical in your body. Sinek defines it as, "The feeling you get when you found something you were looking for or accomplished something you set out to accomplish." Ironically, this chemical is also released during sexual encounters, smoking, alcohol, and gambling. It is very *addictive* when it's unbalanced.

Serotonin has to do with the feeling of pride and status. We, as humans, are social and need the recognition of others. This is the reason we have award ceremonies and all of the pomp and circumstance involved in being in the front of an audience. It's the feeling of status. It's the chemical that surges through the body the moment you graduate from school and celebrate with all the people who helped you accomplish the task.

"The only problem is that this chemical can be tricked, through superficial means," says Sinek. "It's the reason they put the logos on the outside of our clothing. We like the red line on our *Prada* glasses. How good does it feel when you slip on your designer shoes? You can literally feel your confidence rise."[30]

That same feeling occurs in your teen every time they receive some sort of perceived value and status on their life as a product on display for the world. It's also how your teen defines where they fit in the hierarchy of their culture or in their sphere of influence.

In my research with teens, it became very clear that anything that feeds that perception of value and status is something they must consume. It's a learned behavior that's amplified by our sociological need for acceptance. Social media is visual, which means anything that gives them popularity is the target of dopamine.

Some of the teens I interviewed were very candid in their responses of what leads them to post. "When I am bored, I post things of when I went out with my friends. I want people just to see that I went out with my friends even though I might not be out at that moment."

Another teen focused on how social media posts provide comparison after looking at other people online, "If it's somebody that's crying on their kitchen floor on YouTube, it makes you feel good about your life. Like my life's not that bad. It could be worse. But then there are all these people making billions of dollars, living happy lives, and posting they have like fifteen Ferraris in their garage. And you're just like, why is that not me? I can't even afford a bike."

The Stats on Teen Social Media Addiction

- 92% of teens go online daily, and 24% say they go online "almost constantly."
- 76% of teens use social media (81% of older teens, 68% of teens ages 13 and 14).
- 71% of teens use Facebook, 52% use Instagram, 41% use Snapchat, 33% use Twitter, and 14% use Tumblr.
- 77% of parents say their teens get distracted by their devices and don't pay attention when they're together.
- 59% of parents say they feel their teen is addicted to their mobile device.
- 50% of teens say they feel addicted to their mobile device.[31]

I Will Do Anything for "A Like"

Scientists have found that overuse of technology in general, and social media in particular, creates a stimulation pattern similar to the pattern created by other addictive behaviors. Psychological studies prove that receiving "likes" or affirmation on social media activates the same circuits in the teenage brain that are activated by eating chocolate or winning money. "The brain responds to social media the same way it responds to real-life connections, with a release of dopamine—a neurotransmitter that creates feelings of pleasure and works in the reward center of the brain," says Kristin Wilson, MA, LPC, Director of Clinical Outreach at Newport Academy. "Positive reinforcement comes when a teen posts something online and is met with likes, shares, and positive comments from their circle of peers. The rush of dopamine that occurs with this positive feedback creates a 'high.' For some, this can begin the cycle of the need to recreate that feeling with more posts and thus more time on social media."

THE MOMENT YOU SIGN UP FOR SOCIAL MEDIA, YOU BECOME A PRODUCT.

I surveyed a group of teens concerning why people post certain things and this one quote summed up the general thinking: "I use a lot of social media to promote me, and when I think about it, I think, 'Okay, I want people to accept this and accept who I am and what I do.' So really, I use it a lot as a marketing tool. And then, too, just to give insight into my life. Like, 'Hey, look at what I'm doing. Like look who I'm with.'"

My editor's granddaughter posted her picture with a friend on Instagram. This 13-year-old was at her friend's house and modeling a very revealing bikini. Completely unaware of all the potential sexual predators that could be lurking behind fake names and likes, she only thought about her friends seeing and liking her post. Her alarmed grandfather saw the picture and immediately wrote back to her on Instagram and reported what he saw to her parents. Immediately, some very serious conversations happened among the family members and this young girl who was only looking for a few likes on her social media connection.

Other teens often echo similar online pics or comments including wanting to get the opposite sex to think they are cool and wanting to be seen by them. This idea relates back to the same reasons it's easy for teens to be lured by people meaning to do them harm. They are simply seeking some form of validation or where they fit in.

Remember how we talked about dopamine being addictive? Just ask any drug addict what happens when this chemical becomes unbalanced. They will tell you they will do anything to seek another hit of that feeling. This is the reason teens post a certain kind of photo. Let's be honest, adults do it too. We will do almost anything for a "like" on our post!

"Teenagers have always worried about how they measure up: Am I popular? Attractive? Do I fit in? Social media now answers those questions in a very public and quantifiable way. It's not just about the number of 'likes' and online friends a young person has. The data on popularity can be even more granular: how many photos you're 'tagged' in, the level of activity and comments on your posts, how long it takes to accumulate those status markers, and even the 'follow ratio,' that is, how many people you follow versus follow you," says Jennifer Breheny Wallace in the Wall Street Journal article "The Teenage Social-Media Trap."[32]

STATUS EQUALS MOVING UP IN THE HIERARCHY, SO WE BEGIN TO MOLD OURSELVES BASED ON CERTAIN STANDARDS THAT RECEIVE THE MOST ATTENTION.

The same thing goes for trends. I'm sure you can think of one item of clothing that became popular when you were a teenager. More importantly, what did having the "cool" item mean for you as a teenager among your peers?

Social media can also become a coping tool like any other addiction. Just like other "addictions,"the user might not even know they are addicted. If an alcoholic or smoker is feeling stressed, they instantly turn to those things to calm them down. If each "like" or positive post gives teens the shot of dopamine they need, then they will continue to seek that feeling.

Simon Sinek puts it this way, "We have an entire generation of people going through the earliest stressful times of their life with access to a device that will provide them with some sort of instant relief in the palm of their hands."[33]

Since many kids are being given devices at younger ages, they are losing real social coping skills and simply finding value only through social media coping. This addiction is the reason they keep scrolling on a page or keep checking back to see how many people have seen their image. They have learned only a superficial value system of status and it doesn't cost them anything but time. It might cost a little dignity depending on how mature themed the images are, but that perceived value among peers becomes more important.

Your teen has grown up in a world where everything is staged, it's a filter. They can hide how they feel on a post or take a particular self-image that makes it seem as if they are ok, but don't be fooled.

EVERY SINGLE IMAGE THAT IS POSTED BY YOUR CHILD IS A SEARCH FOR VALIDATION IN SOME FORM.

Key Takeaways and Digital Principles

- **The value in social media really comes from two parts, perceived worth and communication.**
- **Every social media platform provides one basic function for the world to see and that's how many followers you have.**
- **On social media, everyone is a product, they just don't know it.**
- **The moment you sign up for social media, you become a product.**
- **Status equals moving up in the hierarchy, so we begin to mold ourselves based on certain standards that receive the most attention.**
- **Every single image that is posted by your child is a search for validation in some form.**

Family Discussion Points

1. Why are you posting?
2. Discuss personal value.
3. Conduct a conversation on what are good and bad pictures.
4. Discuss the consequences of the pictures short and long term.

Notes

Social Media Is Not Real Connection

"Teens and social media addiction are an unfortunate match. In addition, teens seek online experiences for a sense of escape and connection,"

—Nicholas Kardaras
author of *Glow Kids: How Screen Addiction Is Hijacking Our Kids—and How to Break the Trance.*[34]

Life Conversation Question: What are you thinking about and what do you hope to gain from the picture you posted?

Girl 1: "Well, it depends on how I feel at that moment. If I want to post something like a mood I'm feeling or whatever."

Girl 2: "The only time I post things is when I'm bored or when I go out with my friends and I want people just to see that I went out with my friends."

We've created a culture that has lost the true meaning of friendship. They are seeking to be heard by anyone. Because we measure value by "likes or friends," we need to do that to feel good. It connects us to people we don't know. Sometimes the connection runs deep and fast; it is a good time waster, and we can share how we feel, our mood. It's not just one conversation, it's an ongoing conversation.

OFTEN PARENTS FEEL LIKE THEY NEED TO GUESS WHAT IS GOING ON WITH THEIR KIDS OR THEY JUST NEED SPACE.
THAT IS THE WRONG MOVE.

You're the adult! It's okay to help steer your children in the right direction. *Remember, technology changes but principles do not.* Your kids are smarter than you think. They have more access than you did growing up, so they think they know more as digital natives. The truth is, they do in terms of access but having the access doesn't mean they know what to do with it. That's where you come in.

As adults, we don't know everything, so don't fake it. Let your teens know you have a real interest in what's going on in their lives. It's not the 1980s. The excuse you are not good with computers is no longer acceptable. Your life as an adult is crazy and maybe you don't want to learn another thing. However, here is the reality of it all. You take time to know what's going on in the news, right? So, why not invest time to learn the tools that are literally shaping your child's life. Since the world of social media intersects with the real world, (page 9) banning social media or certain technologies simply will not work.

Connected Safety: There is a risk of social marginalization for kids not allowed to socialize in this way. This is the medium that helps them develop in their social circles. It's better for them to understand wise usage over no usage at all. As parents, you may not fully understand everything your child is doing, which is why keeping as much of the lines open as possible is key.

Check the Devices: *New York Times* best-selling author and blogger John Acuff shares a story about how smart device access could potentially put your kids in sticky situations. Acuff's daughters were using two innocent web sites that were about dolls. One site let them email other members of the site with pre-written messages like, 'Have a good day!' or 'Hooray for rainbows.' That's harmless for an eight-year-old. But the other site let them write their own messages. "Without me realizing it, my kids had received their first email address."[35]

John's story reflects the naivety of most parents when it comes to smart devices. If there is an on switch and it has internet access, you need to know more than the name of the device. It's your responsibility to research what the devices can and can't do. From the '90s to the early 2000s, if I wanted to play *Dragon Ball Z* or *Final Fantasy* (videogames) on a *PlayStation* with my friends we had to go over to each other's house, sit in the living room or bedroom, and play; wow, what a crazy idea. Our parents, like many others at the time, only worried about us somehow getting a hold of a game with a mature rating which meant mild blood and maybe a few "bad words." They also had concerns about the amount of time we stayed inside instead of riding our bikes, but overall technology addiction wasn't a major concern. However, this isn't the '90s and kids now have smartphones!

Can you imagine using your phone or game system to play against people in other countries in real time? In fact, most gaming systems require you to go online for the maximum gaming experience.

Parental Guidance Suggested[36]

Dr. Carolyn Jaynes who designs for *Leap Frog*, one of the largest children's educational and entertainment companies believes, "Parents should keep media screens in family areas so that a child's media usage can be monitored, and TVs and computers should be kept out of bedrooms." You can help your child get more out of a smartphone or tablet by sharing in the experience. Engage with your children as they try out a new device or app, asking probing questions and pointing out different aspects of the content.

"It's important to focus on the content and message when making age-appropriate media choices. What children watch and play matters," says Jaynes. She recommends that parents learn to distinguish between educational and entertainment-based content. There definitely is a difference. This particularly comes into play when younger kids are first given access to technology. Oftentimes parents will give their kids a smart device as a form of distraction for hours at a time while the adults are occupied with something else. Understand the content your child is consuming is still influencing their development. Choose content that's going to stimulate their brains in a thoughtful way, teaching them life lessons, not just using the tool as a digital babysitter.

Parental Controls[37]

- **Smartphones and Tablets.** Whether you are an *iPhone* or *Android* user, the company's operating systems offers built-in parental controls for mobile devices. For example, *Google* will let you set limits on your Android phone and your kids' phones. You can also download apps, such as Google's Family Link, to track and control online activity, including text messaging and social media. If you're an Amazon user, *Kindle Fire* tablets come preloaded with Kindle parental controls. **Good to know**: Monitor your kid's social media accounts; you'll need their passwords and user names. **Good for**: Younger kids. Once kids get older, they will either resist any attempt to limit their access or simply figure out a way to defeat what you've restricted.

- **Your device's operating system.** *Microsoft's Windows, Apple's Mac OS*, and *Google Chrome* come with built-in parental controls. To get the most benefits, you need to use the most updated version of the operating system, and each user has to log in under his or her profile.
Good to know: You don't have to pay extra for them, and they apply globally to everything the computer accesses.
Good for: All ages.

- **Web browsers.** Browsers, for example, *Mozilla Firefox*, *Google Chrome*, and *Apple Safari* are the software you use to go on the Internet. Each one offers different ways of filtering out web sites you don't want your kids to visit. Learn how to set restrictions in your browser. **Good to know**: Browsers are free, but if you have more

than one on your machine, you need to enable filters on all of them.
Good for: Younger kids. Older kids—especially very determined ones—can easily defeat browser restrictions either by figuring out your password or simply downloading a new browser.

- **Kids' browsers.** Sometimes called "walled gardens," these are protected environments that fill up your entire screen (so kids can't click out of them). They typically offer games, preapproved web sites, email, and various activities.
  Good to know: Kids' browsers are usually free for the basic version, but cost money for a premium upgrade. They also sometimes display ads or promotional content.
  Good for: Younger kids. Walled gardens are too limiting for older kids who need (or are allowed) greater access to the wider web.

- **Third-party apps and software.** Full-featured parental-control programs, such as *NetNanny* and *Qustodio* let you block web sites, impose screen-time limits, and monitor online activity (for example, which sites your kid visits) on your computer or laptop. Many of these programs also offer added security against malware and viruses and will send you a summary of what your kid does online.
  Good to know: They usually require a monthly subscription fee.
  Good for: Kids of all ages — and especially kids who need a lot of support in following your rules.

- **Home Networking.** There are both hardware and software solutions to control your home network and WiFi. *OpenDNS* is a download that works with your existing router (the device that brings the internet into your home) to filter internet content. *Circle Home* is a device that pairs with your existing router and offers management features such as the ability to pause the internet, create time limits, and add content filters. (Some new *Netgear* routers are also bundling *Circle's* features; contact your service provider for details.)
  Good to know: Mucking around in your network and WiFi settings can be challenging.
  Good for: All ages.[38]

Key Takeaways and Digital Principles

- **Often parents feel like they need to guess what is going on with their kids or they just need space. That is the wrong move.**

Family Discussion Points

1. Parents, what three thing would you like to see your teen do more of? And less of?
2. Ask your teen what are three things involving their technology usage they would like you to do more of? And less of?

Notes

Your House, Your Rules

"No one cares more about your child's well-being and success than you do. In today's digitally-fueled times, that means guiding him or her not just in the real world but in the always-on virtual one as well. Teach your children to use technology in a healthy way and pick up the skills and habits that will make them successful digital citizens. From 2-year-olds who seem to understand the iPad better than you to teenagers who need some (but not too much) freedom, we'll walk you through how to make technology work for your family at each stage of the journey."

—Melanie Pinola

"How (and When) to Limit Kids' Tech Use"[39]

Here are some of the most important things to do when giving your tween/teen a tech device.

Establish Safe Zones. My research shows this tends to be a tough one for many parents. What I mean by this is creating an environment built on understanding that your child is going to make mistakes and you offer a judgment free zone.

I had a parent say to me, "Family meetings are a judgment-free zone. They can openly share anything." They told me that by doing so, their teens have been very open in communicating, even when a girl sent a naked photo to them. The parents calmly explained the ramification of a person's future and even the potential legal trouble of so-called "innocent" photos.

Think of it like seeing a counselor, but with more authority. If you have never been to a counselor, they provide a safe place to share and help you work through your issues by helping you process. The only time they are legally obligated to say something is if the action involves children or if there is a reason to believe you might harm yourself.

Set the Password. Privacy? What privacy? Parents, you might have forgotten but you purchased that phone or electronic device and the "kids" live under your roof. The reality is, privacy is a luxury you provide to them. Smartphones do hold a good amount of personal information and the ability to send money or make purchases. Setting a password is actually one of the first things you are prompted to do when logging in to your device. Keeping them secure from the wrong people is important. *Parents, you are not the wrong people.* What are they hiding that you can't see? This isn't so much a trust issue, it's more that it's your right as a parent to have access.

Set Designated Social Media/Technology Times. Being alone or idleness causes trouble. This principle also applies to television. If you have decided to allow your children to have a smart device, the rules are they can only be used in the public areas of your home. Smart devices will not be allowed in bedrooms or away from where people can see or hear what you are doing. Of course, there are always exceptions to the rules based on your household.

Don't Forbid Dialogue. To this day, I'm a big proponent of "why." Poor parenting says thing like, "Because I'm the mother/father and you do what I say." Establish the ground rules and dialogue about the why behind these concerns. Just because things are "standards" according to society, doesn't mean they have to be in your home. Teens need boundaries; it's how we as people function in society.

Technology and social media have become such an extension of our brains, we always have it with us. People literally spend hours scrolling on an app doing nothing but commenting on another person's photos. I remember in the '90s when *America Online* (AOL) first came out. There were literally timers for the teen login. I remember telling my friends I needed to get off at a specific time. I hated it then but looking back, I can appreciate it. It becomes a time waster. Your teen will not self-regulate so help them by limiting their usage.

Download a Safety App or Use the Built-In Ones. *Apple* has built tools into the iOS—the operating system used by their products—to let parents control the content and apps their children can access.

There are apps available via Android and iPhone that allow you to be notified whenever an app is downloaded. Even if you established communication with your teen, there are apps called ghosting apps. These are designed to look innocent, like a calculator, but will open a profile and secret browser. Why would a person need that? The answer is simple. It is to have a place for sharing bad content. Remember, the phone already has a password; why would a teen or anyone besides the CIA or NSA need some sort of super-secret folder? Here is the trick once an app is downloaded. You should research and find out what the app does, its rating, and how it works.

Get Them to Teach. People like to help others, especially if it's in the same realm of interest. Sign up for some of the same apps your kids are using; be open about it. Ask them to show you how it works and what are some of the new features.

Don't Keep it a Secret. People change their behavior when they know they are being monitored. It's just the nature of people according to Pew Research.[40] Be up front with them, let them know everything they are doing online is being monitored for safety reasons. The goal here is not to trap or catch your children doing something wrong. The goal is protection and also a space to dialogue about what's going on in their lives.

- 18% of Americans who are aware of surveillance programs say they have changed the way they use their email accounts "somewhat" or a "great deal."
- In addition, 17% say they have changed the way they use search engines.
- 15% of those interviewed say they have changed the way they use social media.
- 15% say they have changed the way they use their cell phones.
- 13% of app users say they have changed the way they use mobile apps.

- 13% say they have changed the way they use text messages.
- 9% say they have changed the way they use their landline phone.[41]

KEY TAKEAWAYS AND DIGITAL PRINCIPLES

- **Establish Safe Zones.**
- **Set the Password.**
- **Set Designated Social Media Times.**
- **Don't Forbid Dialogue.**
- **Download a Safety App or Use the Built-in Ones.**
- **Have Them Teach You About the Device and Apps They Are Using.**
- **Don't Keep Monitoring a Secret.**

Family Discussion Points

1. Set aside time each week to share one-on-one time together.
2. Kids, take a moment to affirm a few things you like about your parents.
3. Parents, take a moment to affirm a few things you like about your kids.

Notes

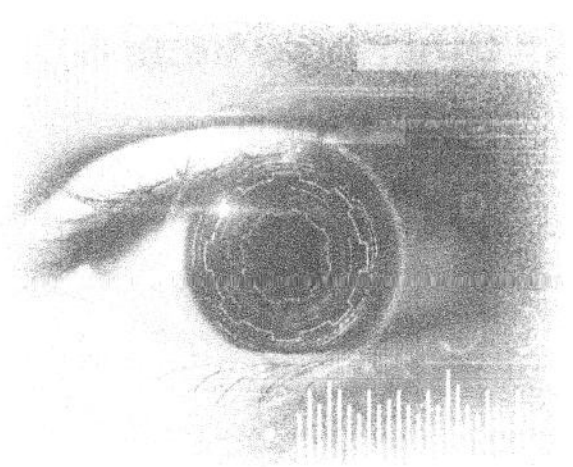

Final Word

After reading about all of the unforeseen digital pitfalls your kids are going through you might feel a bit overwhelmed. Let me just provide some encouragement by reminding you that when you first became a parent you had the same feelings. You adjusted and were able to get through those challenges, this is just *another* one of those challenges waiting to be conquered. Parenting is a full-time job and often we don't stand back to observe *how the work we have already put in is paying off.* Take three deep breaths (seriously do it right now) and repeat after me, I am a GOOD PARENT and I DON'T OWN every decision my teen makes. I guide them to the best of my ability but (insert their name) is/are an individual(s) and there are certain things they are going to learn on their own.

In a printed book like this, it can be difficult to remember the important comments, facts, and principles or takeaways. In order to help you, I have created an index of these important "Digital Principles" for you to remember.

Review the endnotes and links I have listed as well. Educate yourself. Involve family members in the discussion questions. Remember, the technology isn't the problem...or evil. It's how we use or abuse it that must be weighed. Technology is simply a way to enhance our lives and the way we communicate. It does not replace the classic 5 "Love Languages" between parents and kids:

- **Words of Affirmation**
- **Physical Touch**
- **Receiving Gifts**
- **Acts of Service**
- **Quality Time**[42]

You already have the life experience, now you have an additional tool to use as *technology changes but principles do not*, on this continual journey called parenting.

Postscript

Important Takeaways & Digital Principles for You to Remember

1. Every family member should know what devices and digital platforms all the other family members are using, along with the boundaries for using them.
2. Media shapes and influences the mind-sets of kids.
3. Media contributes significantly to shaping a kid's perspective on life. For many tweens and teens, media is the primary potter shaping the vessel's (kid's) values, hopes, dreams, desires, passions, and even spiritual understandings.
4. Kids are motivated by media to buy stuff. What your kids spend money on indicates not only their needs but also their desires and values.
5. "Cool hunting" was all about a kind of revolution that sets that earlier paradigm aside and says, in fact, it has to do with the influence held by those who have the respect and admiration and trust of their friends.
6. Companies look for the 20 percent, the trendsetters, that are going to influence the other 80 percent.
7. In short, executives don't know what cool is, but they hire "cool" to shape your kids.
8. Companies use Trojan Horses to determine how to sell to your kids.

9. Remember, unrestricted mobile access is like a sewage line, with all kinds of content. A couple of misspellings might take your child down a place they don't want to go.
10. In the real world, your child might be aware of "stranger danger," but online anonymity provides a false sense of security.
11. When there is the ability to delete or hide a conversation, there comes a great likelihood to participate in risky behavior.
12. Your feelings are not that different from the people that came before you.
13. The key principle here is communication and sharing yourself and some of your past experiences with your child.
14. Psychological research suggests effective communication can be summed up in "The Three C's" of communication: Context, Cluster, and Congruence.
15. Psychologists suggest over 80 percent of communication is nonverbal.[43] However, when communicating through a device, these factors of communication are primarily erased.
16. When looking at a pixel on a screen, the chemical emotions are real, but the consequences are not tangible.
17. Kids think the rules of the real world don't apply online.
18. The value in social media really comes from two parts, perceived worth and communication.

19. Every social media platform provides one basic function for the world to see and that's how many followers you have.
20. On social media, everyone is a product; they just don't know it.
21. The moment you sign up for social media, you become a product.
22. Status equals moving up in the hierarchy, so we begin to mold ourselves based on certain standards that receive the most attention.
23. Every single image that is posted by your child is a search for validation in some form.
24. Often parents feel like they need to guess what is going on with their kids or they just need space. That is the wrong move.
25. Establish Safe Zones.
26. Set the Password.
27. Set Designated Social Media Times.
28. Don't Forbid Dialogue.
29. Download a Safety App or Use the Built-in Ones.
30. Have Them Teach You About the Device and Apps They Are Using.
31. Don't Keep Monitoring a Secret.

Endnotes

[1] *The 7 Habits of Highly Effective People: Powerful Lessons in Personal Change* by Stephen R. Covey.
[2] https://www.brainyquote.com/quotes/bill_gates_626104?src=t_social_media
[3] https://en.wikipedia.org/wiki/Social_media#Definition_and_classification
[4] Technoself studies - Wikipedia https://en.wikipedia.org/wiki/Technoself
[5] Merriam-Webster's Collegiate Dictionary
[6] *The Impact of Social Media on Relationships,* by Rachel Kitson, Ph.D. October 16, 2017
[7] http://www.pewinternet.org/2018/03/01/social-media-use-in-2018/
[8] http://www.pewinternet.org/2018/03/01/social-media-use-in-2018/
[9] https://www.wired.com/2015/01/a-teenagers-view-on-social-media/
[10] http://www.snopes.com/business/market/mandms.asp
[11] https://tinyurl.com/y8624g2r
[12] https://www.creditdonkey.com/teenage-consumer-spending-statistic.html
[13] http://www.pbs.org/wgbh/pages/frontline/shows/cool/etc/script.html
[14] https://www.commonsensemedia.org/marketing-to-kids/what-is-the-impact-of-advertising-on-teens
[15] Common Sense is the nation's leading nonprofit organization dedicated to improving the lives of kids and families by providing the trustworthy information, education, and independent voice they need to thrive in the 21st century.
[16] Russakoff, D. Marketers following youth trends to the bank, "The Washington Post," April 19, 1999.
[17] Wilcox, B., Cantor, J., Dowrick, P., Kunkel, D., Linn, S., & Palmer, E. (2004). "Report of the APA Task Force on Advertising and Children: Recommendations."
[18] https://nypost.com/2017/11/14/rise-in-teen-suicide-connected-to-social-media-popularity-study/
[19] www1.cbn.com/cbnnews/us/2015/October/Grieving-Mother-Warns-of-Online-Predators
[20] http://woodtv.com/2015/02/02/sexual-predator-warns-parents-about-kik-app/
[21]https://brainconnection.brainhq.com/2013/03/20/decision-making-is-still-awork-in-progress-for-teenagers/

[22] Read: Begley, S. February 28, 2000. "Getting Inside a Teen Brain." *Newsweek*.
[23] https://peerteachproject.weebly.com/the-5-cs.html
[24] https://thriveglobal.com/stories/how-social-media-affects-our-ability-to-communicate/
[25] May/June 2013 Issue, "Social Media and Interpersonal Communication," by Maura Keller, Social Work Today Vol. 13 No. 3 p. 10
[26] https://www.psychologytoday.com/blog/beyond-words/201109/is-nonverbal-communication-numbers-game
[27] May/June 2013 Issue, "Social Media and Interpersonal Communication," by Maura Keller, *Social Work Today* Vol. 13 No. 3 p. 10
[28] https://www.psychologytoday.com/blog/beyond-words/201109/is-nonverbal-communication-numbers-game
[29] https://childmind.org/article/how-using-social-media-affects-teenagers/
[30] (https://www.youtube.com/watch?v=ReRcHdeUG9Y)
[31] Sources: Pew Research Center and Common Sense Media
[32] Sources: Pew Research Center and Common Sense Media https://www.wsj.com/articles/the-teenage-social-media-trap-1525444767
[33] (https://www.youtube.com/watch?v=ReRcHdeUG9Y)
[34] https://www.newportacademy.com/resources/mental-health/teens-social-media-addiction/
[35] http://theparentcue.org
[36] http://www.pbs.org/parents/childrenandmedia/article-when-introduce-child-smartphone-tablet.html
[37] https://www.commonsensemedia.org/blog/everything-you-need-to-know-about-parental-controls
[38] https://www.commonsensemedia.org/blog/everything-you-need-to-know-about-parental-controls
[39] https://www.nytimes.com/guides/smarterliving/family-technology
[40] http://www.pewinternet.org/2015/03/16/how-people-are-changing-their-own-behavior/
[41] http://www.pewinternet.org/2015/03/16/how-people-are-changing-their-own-behavior/
[42] Gary Chapman https://www.5lovelanguages.com/
[43] https://www.psychologytoday.com/blog/beyond-words/201109/is-nonverbal-communication-numbers-game

About the Author

CALEB KINCHLOW is an Emmy Award-winning Host, Digital Lifestyle Expert, and Multimedia Producer with a focus on technology and youth empowerment. A few of his most notable assignments and awards have included, Technology Blogger for The Huffington Post; two Emmys, one as the Host of an entertainment-education series for NASA (NASA360) and as the Creator/Host for the Digital Download technology show. Caleb also received a Parent's Choice Education Award as the Host of Colonial Williamsburg's Emmy Award-winning live call-in program (HERO Live), syndicated on PBS and streaming in over a thousand schools across the country.

He previously served as the Fine Arts Director for Youth Entertainment Studios in Norfolk, Virginia. The (YES) program was designed to use fine arts as a catalyst to teach inner-city students life skills. Caleb also travels across the country motivating students of all ages with his central message, "You Are Born For Greatness." Caleb's sessions focus on communicating the importance of understanding one's purpose and functioning at the level of greatness they were designed for.

Caleb holds an M.A. from Regent University in Digital Media, a B.S. from Southeastern University in Broadcast Television, and a Minor in Film from The Los Angeles Film Studies Center. He and his wife, Amanda, currently have two incredible kids, Jailyn and Demarcus.

calebkinchlow.com